NAVIGATE

Understanding the Five
Types of People

Navigate courageously!

NAVIGATE

Understanding the Five Types of People

Dr. Sherene McHenry

The People IQ Expert™

Reach Higher Press

Navigate: Understanding the Five Types of People

2nd Edition

Copyright © 2019 by

Sherene McHenry

Book and Cover Design:

Marty Somberg / sombergdesign.com

Reach Higher Press

ISBN 978-0-9824688-2-1

Reach Higher Press titles may be purchased in bulk for educational, business, fund-raising or sales promotional use. For information, please email SpecialMarkets@ReachHigherPress.com

Publisher's Note:

This book is not intended as a substitute for counseling, medical, financial or legal advice. If expert assistance is required, the services of a competent professional should be sought.

To Mom and Dad,
You shine as brilliantly as any lighthouse.
Thank you for living your values,
loving extravagantly and empowering me to
navigate my way to a life I truly love.

CONTENTS

Introduction

What would your life be like if you uncovered new ways to understand and interact with people that enabled you to be happier, empowered you to create healthier relationships and positioned you for greater satisfaction and success?

I have been fascinated by people as long as I can remember. Like searching for buried treasure, I've hunted for what I, and people like you, want and need in life and relationships.

Wired to be helpful and wanting everyone happy, I gave my first relationship advice to an adult before I was licensed to drive. Not surprisingly, it was ignored.

Lacking knowledge, I painfully steered my ship aground. Perhaps you have too. Knowing I needed help, I entered counseling in my mid 20s. Learning to create healthier relationships and to tell myself and others the truth about what I wanted and needed, significantly enhanced my life.

Inspired to help others, I earned my doctorate in Counseling, then invested almost two decades as a graduate professor. The differences in how my students approached their education and interacted with others intrigued and confused me.

Shockingly, not every student was highly motivated to learn. Not every student wanted to be there. Not every student, or colleague for that matter, cared about relationships.

Despite their differences, like a hampered builder using only a hammer, I treated them as though they were all wired the same. Frustrating for me and for them.

After running into the same brick wall one too many times, I finally figured out that people are **different** and therefore required differing approaches and strategies. My relationships and success improved, and my life became happier and easier. Yours will too.

A huge fan of Dr. Gary Chapman's *The Five Love Languages*, I longed to discover something equally simple and profound. I didn't just want to effectively impact students, I wanted to follow in Chapman's footsteps and transform lives and relationships around the globe.

Through decades of studying, observing and conducting interviews, I've uncovered five types of people: High Flyers, Steady Gliders, Lackers, Slackers and Hackers. Each possesses distinctive qualities, unique motivations and divergent needs. What a difference knowing how to navigate each type has made.

The good news is, you don't have to make the same mistakes I have. You don't have to repeatedly run into the same wall. You don't have to get an advanced degree. You don't have to spend decades analyzing interactions.

Like GPS mapping out the quickest route to your destination, this book will empower you to skillfully navigate the five types of people, enhance your life and relationships and steer your way to greater success.

With great anticipation,

Sherene

CHAPTER ONE

Navigate Your Way To Healthier Relationships And A Happier Life

Do people ever baffle you? Have you ever been left holding the bag after someone said they would do something but didn't follow through? Have you witnessed or been on the receiving end of a tirade? Do you repeatedly get stuck doing other people's jobs?

People come in all shapes and sizes. Many are trustworthy, reliable, hardworking, helpful, giving and kind. Some fade into the woodwork. Others procrastinate. Still others are takers. There are even people who deliberately cause drama and delight in destruction and deception.

Relationships would be easy to navigate if everyone was committed, reliable and trying to make the world a better place. But everyone isn't.

Consider the 2017 Gallup Poll of American employees. Only 33% self-reported being actively engaged and committed to their work and work place. The vast majority, 51%, indicated being passively disengaged.

A terrifying 16% reported being actively disengaged and trying to cause problems.

I believe the percentages to be similar outside of the workplace. If you look, you will mostly find one third of people engaged and working hard to make things better, half coasting on the coattails of others, and far too many actively trying to cause problems.

You steer into stormy seas each time you fail to recognize and acknowledge there are people content to create chaos or to do as little as they possibly can.

Unless you are completely isolated, you interact with people continuously. The stakes get bigger and the interactions more numerous when you live, work with or lead others.

There are five types of people you will continually encounter, and you must learn to navigate if you want to enjoy optimal success. They include:

High Flyers - Driven, get it done now people who are highly reliable, conscientious and competent. At highest risk for burnout.

Steady Gliders - Reliable, conscientious and competent individuals who, although they may carry heavy burdens, rarely call attention to themselves and are often overlooked.

Lackers - Individuals missing either a skill set or mind set which negatively impedes their performance and success.

Slackers - People who tend to procrastinate and coast on the work and generosity of others.

Hackers - Individuals actively trying to cause problems.

If you want to enjoy happier, healthier relationships and enhanced success you must effectively navigate yourself and others. As Allen Watts said, "The wake doesn't drive the ship."

What works with highly driven, internally motivated individuals is counterproductive for individuals who march to a different beat. Similarly, what works with someone who cares about relationships backfires with individuals who don't.

The following chapters dive into each of the five types of people and provide examples for applying what you are learning. We also explore the pitfalls of each type.

Once you understand yourself, your needs and your pitfalls, it becomes far easier to navigate toward and manage long-term success. The same applies to understanding and interacting with others.

Let's go!

CHAPTER 2

Full Steam Ahead: High Flyers

Are "reliable", "conscientious" and "dedicated" words synonymous with your name and reputation? Do you start a new task immediately and only fully feel settled once it is finished? If you can't do something well, would you rather not do it at all?

Are you driven to deliver? Do you take great pride in your work? Do you bring your A-game to everything you do? Would you rather run yourself ragged than let someone down?

If so, you are an achiever. A natural born, get things done, High Flyer whose drive, talents and hard work make you highly sought after in and out of the workplace.

Unfortunately, the traits that make you a rock star can also be your greatest weaknesses. In excess, your integrity and dedication to duty enable and embolden others to inadvertently overload your capacity or intentionally exploit your work ethic.

You can also get so entangled in serving, pleasing and

taking care of others that you fail to take care of yourself. Then, instead of captaining your life, you become the pooper scooper of someone else's parade.

My mother is a prime example of a driven to excel, High Flyer. Taking great pride in her work, when she says she will do something, she delivers. Whether a task is big or small, she gives her all. Like other purebred High Flyers, she's been that way since she was a child.

Practicing long hours, she became an accomplished pianist as a child. Despite the fact that she had to play it with a piece of string until her arm grew long enough to reach the notes, she also mastered the trombone.

In high school she was class officer, varsity cheerleader, homecoming queen, star of the senior play and valedictorian. Speeding through college, my mother started teaching fulltime at the tender age of 20.

I remember her working long evenings and weekends throughout my childhood. Her classroom was beautiful. Her lessons were creative. Her students excelled.

Because she was so conscientious and good at her job she was pressured into becoming principal when the need arose. In High Flyer fashion, she transformed her school into a "showcase" for visiting dignitaries, became the superintendent's "go to" worker bee, created new manuals, clarified procedures, and ensured that each child and parent felt welcomed and valued.

> It is imperative to set High Flyers up for long-term success or you risk losing them to exhaustion and burnout.

Like other High Flyers who haven't learned to say no, my mother became a victim of her success and work ethic. Loaded up with more and more projects, burnout began to loom. Exhaustion finally drove her to say "enough". She packed up her office and went back to doing what she loved, teaching students how to read.

While she still enjoyed teaching, her energy never fully returned. She retired the very day she became eligible. She still gets stopped by parents, former students and colleagues almost every time she's out.

Not A Natural Born High Flyer?

If you, like me, approach the world differently, don't despair. While it isn't wired into your DNA like it is into a natural born High Flyer, you can achieve great success and become a High Flyer in your **chosen** endeavors.

You achieve High Flyer status with others by consistently honoring your commitments, doing things well and delivering on time. You achieve High Flyer status in your life by developing and utilizing your gifts, engaging in your passions and working in your sweet spot as much as possible.

> Embrace your humanity, grow and
> treat yourself with the kindness
> you extend to others.

Navigate To Success

It is imperative to set High Flyers up for long-term success. Success that transcends work and fulfilling commitments. Success that affords them time to enjoy life and relationships. Success that enables them to avoid burnout and maintain their health.

We'll start by examining what High Flyers can and need to do to bring out the best in themselves. Then we'll look at what others can do to enhance their relationships with and bring out the best in High Flyers.

Navigating Tips For High Flyers:

At risk for being overworked, overloaded and burning out, it is imperative that you advocate for and take care of yourself. Here are things you can begin doing today to navigate your way to a happier life, healthier relationships and even greater success.

1. **Make excellence your gold standard.** Doing things with excellence is attainable and worthy of your efforts. Chasing perfection, on the other hand, squanders precious resources, causes great frustration

and yields little reward. Send the terrible task master of perfectionism packing. You and everyone around you will be far happier.

2. **Grant yourself permission to be human and make mistakes.** Although you have a strong desire and drive to do things right and not let others including yourself down, you are human. You will make mistakes. Mistakes aren't catastrophes or the end of the world, they are simply invitations to learn and grow wiser.

When you make a mistake don't beat yourself up, berate your intelligence, or hold back in fear of making another mistake. Embrace your humanity, grow and treat yourself with the kindness you extend to others.

If this is an area of struggle for you, I encourage you to read Carol Dweck's *Mindset*. You'll never again look at mistakes as something to be avoided at all costs.

3. **Say yes sparingly.** Once you say yes, you're committed. As it's almost impossible for you to go back on your word, it's imperative you exercise great judgement on what you agree to do personally and professionally. Say yes when:

   a. You are ***truly*** the only person who can do it based on your skills and knowledge base.

b. It is an actual emergency and requires all hands on deck to weather the storm.

c. Doing so will help position you to achieve your hopes and dreams.

d. You want to do it and have the energy, time and other needed resources.

e. You can do it cheerfully and without resentment. If you can't, protect yourself and the relationship by graciously declining.

Model yourself after the High Flyer who recently said, "I can only do so much, and I'm no longer willing to stretch myself too thin. I pick and choose when and where to be a High Flyer based on my passions. I may help with something else, but its success won't be dependent on me."

4. **Say no frequently.** You know the saying, "If you want something done, give it to a busy person." I don't know anyone busier or more unhappy than a High Flyer unwilling to say no.

Because you're hardwired to deliver and do outstanding work, people are always going to want to give you jobs. You must protect yourself and your resources by saying no. Politely navigate unwanted requests with the following replies:

a) No.

b) No thank you.

c) That doesn't/won't work for me.

d) Thanks for thinking of me, but I need to say no.

e) I'm flattered to be asked but my plate is full. You may want to ask "insert name of a Slacker."

f) I can help you with that "next week, next month, next year…"

There is a trick to having your "no" respected and accepted. Say it seriously and refrain from offering an explanation. Bite your tongue if you must, but don't say a word while you wait for their reply.

I recently keynoted at a conference and was talking to an attendee later in the day. She proudly reported she'd put what she learned into action and had just told her boss no without giving an explanation. She was thrilled that his reply was a simple, "OK."

5. **Release guilt.** You may feel guilty saying no. The good news is guilt generally disappears anywhere between 15 minutes to three days. Resentment, on the other hand, grows faster than barnacles on a boat.

Navigate your long-term well-being by picking guilt over resentment every time.

6. **Speak up and send distress signals early.** Because you do great work without complaining, people generally have no idea how much you're doing until you're about to run your ship aground. When tasks and responsibilities are heaped on you, don't suffer silently or buckle under the weight.

Follow the lead of my good friend and mentor, Dr. Terry Rawls. He maintains an ongoing list of current responsibilities and projects.

Ensuring his boss stays aware of what he's doing, he brings it to their meetings and briefly discusses his progress. If asked to take on additional tasks he says, "While I'm happy to help, my plate is overflowing. What would you like for me to remove from my list?"

If you're carrying the heavy load at home, initiate a similar conversation and ask for their help.

Healthy, high functioning individuals will work with you to lessen your overload. Hopefully you'll hear, "I had no idea how much you were doing. Let's redistribute some of these tasks and get you down to a manageable amount."

On the flip side, Lackers, Slackers and Hackers (covered in later chapters) have a vested interest in

> When tasks and responsibilities are heaped on you, don't suffer silently or buckle under the weight.

you continuing to do more than your share. Be prepared for them to respond in keeping with their type.

If someone doesn't care that you are overburdened or their hands are tied, you'll need to determine what you are and aren't willing to do in both the short and long-term.

7. **Tell yourself the truth.** As Maya Angelou exhorted, "When people tell you who they are, believe them."

Read the chapters on Lackers, Slackers and Hackers. Ask them to do better. Their responses will tell you who they are. Refuse to enable under-functioning by doing their work and life tasks.

8. **Take care of yourself.** Working overtime, missing a few hours of sleep and a skipping an occasional meal won't sink your ship. Routinely working the equivalent of almost two full-time jobs, consistently working through lunch and regularly sacrificing sleep so you can get everything done is another matter entirely.

You sail toward stormy seas when you fail to take care of yourself physically, emotionally or spiritually.

9. **Schedule time for fun.** You are a planner and are likely to live by the adage, "You get to play once your work is done." As I'm sure you're well aware, your work will never be fully finished, and there will **always** be jobs calling your name.

   Navigate your way to increased energy and a more satisfying life by intentionally scheduling time for yourself and the things that you enjoy doing. For optimal results, schedule something fun at least once a week.

   Additionally, ensure you always have something scheduled that you're looking forward to such as a vacation, an evening out or a special event. You'll be energized and uplifted just thinking about the fun you'll have.

   In order to ensure this actually happens, schedule fun and down time on your calendar. Then, honor your commitments to yourself as highly as you honor those to others.

10. **Recognize you are enough.** You don't have to earn approval or perform to be worthy. You are worthy because you exist. End of story.

While you might struggle with feeling like a bad person when saying no or making time for yourself, it is ultimately up to you to be the captain of your life. Navigate being a High Flyer well and you will enjoy the rewards of enhanced success, increased joy and greater life satisfaction.

High Flyer Lifelines:

If you are blessed to have a High Flyer in your life, I'm sure you already know that telling them to "relax" or that something "isn't that big a deal" is counterproductive.

While their unwillingness to take a break, relax or lower their standards can be confusing, here are concrete things you can begin doing today to ensure High Flyers are free to soar:

1. **Monitor for overload and burnout.** Like ducks serenely gliding on a lake, most High Flyers are paddling furiously under water. Before giving them a new task, assignment or additional responsibilities, find out what's on their to do list. Additionally, keep an eye out for how many hours they are already working on a daily and weekly basis.

   Burning out your hardest worker is akin to carelessly running a boat aground. It's costly, often catastrophic and entirely avoidable.

2. **Refrain from rewarding them with more work.**
   When High Flyers are given a task, they like to start
   immediately and have a hard time fully relaxing until
   the job is finished. Instead of immediately piling on
   more work, create space for them to breathe, relax
   and bask in the satisfaction of having completed a job.

   In personal relationships, steer a High Flyer toward
   success by insisting they engage in an activity they
   enjoy. For example, take them out or give them a gift
   certificate for something they like to do.

   If you are their boss, send them home early or insist
   they take a two-hour lunch. In the middle or upon
   completion of a long-term project, give them a day off
   or long weekend with firm instructions not to work.

   Use your creativity and work within your system to
   build in breaks for High Flyers that other employees
   are taking at the front end or in the middle of
   completing a task.

   Whether in or out of the workplace, don't let jobs pile
   up for High Flyers while they are gone. Instead of
   returning relaxed, they will feel as though they have
   been punished for being away.

3. **Jettison tasks that others can do.** Delegate tasks
   that other people can do. For example, when my
   mom was in grad school my brother, sister and I each
   prepared dinner one night a week. While meals were

> When you do a task for a High Flyer,
> do it well. Otherwise, they feel they would
> have been better off doing it themselves.

never gourmet, we were all fed. More importantly, Mom's time and energy were freed up.

4. **Distribute jobs fairly.** It is colossally unfair and demotivating for one person to carry the lion's share of the work. Resentment builds and spills over when one person is working extra hard while others are coasting, playing and resting.

5. **Do your share without having to be asked.** Refrain from taking advantage of a High Flyer's generosity, work ethic and drive. When you step up and carry your load, you not only earn their respect and gratitude, you also earn their loyalty.

6. **Do things well.** When you do a task for a High Flyer, do it well. Otherwise, they feel they would have been better off doing it themselves.

7. **Get things done on time and early when possible.** High Flyers feel best when a task is done. When they can trust you to deliver results on time, they feel safe which frees them to focus on their own work, life and dreams.

8. **Don't pile on jobs.** When possible, only give them one new job at a time. When you must give them multiple jobs, prioritize them and take into account what they are already doing. When possible, take things off their plate or move them to the bottom of the list for another time.

9. **Refrain from giving them last minute assignments.** High Flyers are planners. They know what they need to do and how much time it will take them. Giving them a "get it done right now assignment" throws them off their game. They can do it, but you are headed for stormy seas if you ask them to do so on a regular basis.

Each time you protect and refrain from overburdening a High Flyer, you set them up for long-term satisfaction and success.

Sunny skies and smooth sailing await!

CHAPTER 3

Uncharted Depths: Steady Gliders

Are you reliable, conscientious and competent? Do you show up, faithfully fulfill your commitments and leave work behind when you walk out the door?

Do you have a low need to draw attention to yourself? Do you prefer a supporting role over being the upfront face or established leader? Do you sometimes get overlooked for something you know you could easily do if given the chance?

Are you laid back by nature? While you work hard, are relationships and other things more important to you than reaching the top of the career or social ladder? Do you ever question if you're ambitious enough?

If so, you are a Steady Glider. First cousins of High Flyers, you are an often unsung hero who prefers to fly under the radar. While you do a great job when called upon, you'd rather be the person keeping the ship's engine running smoothly than be the one giving out the orders.

> Your strengths and gifts are greatly needed in today's world. You are not broken or deficient. Value yourself, you are enough.

My sister is a prototype Steady Glider. She's hardworking, smart, well-educated and accomplished. While capable and desiring to be involved and make a difference, she's never aspired to be president of an organization. She'd rather serve as a committee member.

Nor does she desire to be director of her department. She enjoys doing her job. And, she highly appreciates being able to leave work behind when the day is done. She lives her values.

Navigate To Success

Sometimes invisible and overlooked, it is imperative to set Steady Gliders up for success. Success that recognizes their skills and talents. Success that respects their values. Success that honors the important contributions they bring to relationships and the workplace.

We'll start by looking at what Steady Gliders can and need to do in order to bring out the best in themselves. Then we'll look at how others can enhance their relationships with and bring out the best in Steady Gliders.

Navigation Tips for Steady Gliders:

As a Steady Glider you are at high risk for lacking confidence and underestimating the significance of your contributions, talents and strengths. Because of your laid-back nature, you are also in jeopardy of being pushed into doing things you don't want to do by people who think they know what is best for you.

Lastly, because you don't regularly call attention to yourself or toot your own horn, you are also in danger of being undervalued and overlooked when new opportunities arise.

The following are tips to guide you to a happier life and healthier relationships that provide more of what you want and less of what you don't.

1. **Know that you are enough.** In a world that tends to narrowly define success as achievement, being driven and striving for more, you march to the beat of a different drum.

   You are different than, not less than. Your strengths and gifts are greatly needed in today's world. You are not broken or deficient. Value yourself, you are enough.

2. **Value what you bring to the table.** Like many Steady Gliders, you may devalue what you bring to the table in and out of the workplace. When you underestimate

> Pursue your passions and interests.
> Doing so will fill you with energy,
> purpose and pride.

your worth, you signal others to undervalue it as well. Even worse, it causes others to underestimate how much you are doing.

Whether in your personal or professional life, you grease the engines and keep things running smoothly. You get the job done. You pull people together. You anchor relationships. You lead the way in helping people get along.

What you bring to the table is vital. Act like the valuable contributor you are and others will respond accordingly.

3. **Define success on your own terms.** While it's important to you to do things well, striving for perfection and achieving external success aren't your primary motivators.

Clarify your definition of success based on your values. Then, regardless of external pressures and messages, set your course toward your desired destination.

While not everyone has the luxury, many Steady Gliders have stepped out of the workplace to raise their children. Others have turned down promotions to stay close to family. Still others have chosen to forgo opportunities rather than uproot their children until they are out of school.

4. **Recognize your passions often lie outside of work.** While you are similar in that you are reliable, conscientious and competent, you are naturally more laid back and relationally oriented than your High Flyer cousins.

   You strive to live a harmonious, balanced life filled with meaningful contributions, rich relationships and time to enjoy the rewards of your labor.

   Whether in or out of the workplace, pursue your passions and interests. Doing so will fill you with energy, purpose and pride. It will also provide you with the fuel needed to fully engage in your life and relationships.

5. **Be true to yourself.** Refuse to let well-intentioned High Flyers or anyone else push you into the life they want you to live.

> Rather than allowing others to hijack your life, ask for what you want and need.

I know far too many Steady Gliders whose High Flyer parents, spouses or bosses, with good intent, push them beyond where they want to go. Even after they've said no repeatedly, some are still being told that who they are and what they value and do isn't enough.

If you are unable to provide for your family or your needs or you are barely getting by on what you make, you may need to consider extra hours or a job change. Being pressed into making more for the sake of more money and to keep your time fully occupied is an entirely different matter.

Deliberately staying out of the rat race is an honorable choice. Carving out a life that affords you time to nurture and enjoy relationships, serve your community and enjoy life is admirable. Living your passions inspires and invites others to do the same.

6. **Find your voice.** While "go along to get along" appears to work as a strategy for avoiding conflict, you give away your power when you stay silent. Rather than allowing others to hijack your life, ask for what you need and want.

Additionally, tolerating bad behavior and scurrying around to ensure others are happy at your expense is akin to trying to bail out a boat with a bucket. It doesn't work. Frustration and resentment build. You will blow up and then be forced to deal with the wreckage.

> Refuse to passively wait to
> be given things.

7. **Speak with confidence.** You possess wisdom and
   have great ideas. Whether sharing your thoughts
   or asking for what you need, don't undermine
   yourself by tentatively weakening your stance.

   Refrain from starting with a disqualifier such as, "I'm
   not positive, but I think I want…" "I know I'm not the
   most knowledgeable, but…" "I haven't been here
   long, but…" "I may be wrong, but…" You give away
   your power each time you say "but" before stating
   what you think, need or want.

   Like you, I sometimes lack confidence concerning
   my needs, ideas and decisions. When I stand in my
   power and refrain from being tentative, people
   take me more seriously.

   You greatly increase your likelihood of being supported
   and having your positions accepted when you speak
   with confidence.

8. **Ask for what you want and need.** As a Steady
   Glider, you may be lacking in the "ask for what you
   want" department. Refuse to passively wait to be
   given things. As Saint James eloquently said, "You
   have not because you ask not."

> You are enough. The world needs you and what you bring to the table. Value yourself. Believe in yourself. Be true to yourself. Find your voice.

Captain your life by being proactive. If there is something you want, ask for it. When an appealing assignment comes up at work, throw your hat into the ring.

In your efforts to keep everyone happy, don't make the mistake of asking others for their opinion when you know what you want. Confidently state what you would like. Once you quit giving away your power, you'll be amazed at how often people will support your choices.

While it takes a great deal of courage to ask for what you want, doing so is imperative as people aren't mind readers. You are far more likely to get things when you request them. You are courageous, deserving and strong. Speak up.

When you don't get what you want, don't despair, go silent or quit asking in the future. Stay persistent. While being told no isn't fun, you are resilient. You are powerful. Keep asking for what you need and want. I am confident you will be pleasantly surprised at what you receive.

9. Say no. While it may be uncomfortable, it is imperative you say no to things that don't fit or aren't right for you. You are not a bad person, selfish or inconsiderate when you say no.

It is up to you to politely decline being pushed into something someone else thinks is best for you. Without providing an explanation and saying it like you mean it, utilize the following responses already suggested to High Flyers to avoid being tossed about by the whims, wants and needs of others:

a) No.

b) No thank you.

c) That doesn't/won't work for me.

d) Thanks for thinking of me, but I need to say no.

e) I'm flattered to be asked but my plate is full. You may want to check with "insert name of a Slacker."

f) I can help you with that "next week, next month, next year..."

You are enough. The world needs you and what you bring to the table. Value yourself. Believe in yourself. Be true to yourself. Find your voice. Captain your life and you will reach your desired destination.

Lifelines for Steady Gliders:

While Steady Gliders share many characteristics of High Flyers, they are decidedly unique. Preferring to fly under the radar and driven by different values, these reliable, conscientious and hardworking individuals get things done with little fanfare. It is imperative they be better understood.

Use the following tips to ensure Steady Gliders feel valued and positioned for success: .

1. **Respect their values.** Steady Gliders aren't driven to achieve perfection or continually striving for bigger, better, more prestigious things. They rarely desire the spotlight or top billing. They certainly aren't lazy.

   Don't try to turn them into someone they aren't. You risk throttling their best qualities when you fail to recognize and respect them as unique and gifted individuals.

   Bring out the best in them by honoring their contributions and hard work. Refrain from making them feel guilty for valuing relationships, service to others and a life outside of work.

2. **Encourage them to follow their passions and pursue their dreams.** Listen to what they want and support their desires. While they may differ from yours, their wants and needs are equally valid.

> What you consider a great
> job might be their version
> of a nightmare.

Inspire them to achieve by cheering them on as they contemplate taking risks.

Steady Gliders often lack confidence, so it's particularly important not to rain on their parade or be a Negative Nelly. Instead of immediately telling them, "That won't work" ask them, "How will that work?"

Don't squelch their dreams with comments such as, "Can you make any money with that?" and "Why did you bother getting a degree if you weren't going to get a good job?"

What you consider a good job might be their version of a nightmare. Respect that they value things other than making more money when it comes to career and life decisions. They know how they are wired. Trust that they will figure out what they need to do to make a living.

Encourage them to achieve their dreams and create a life they love. You'll be rewarded with a far happier person and may even be surprised at their success.

> Sometimes all a Steady Glider needs is a bit of encouragement as they take on something new and challenging. Gently remind them of the skills they possess.

3. Recognize and reward your unsung heroes.
While Steady Gliders can easily be overlooked, failing to recognize and honor their hard work and dependability is demotivating.

Despite the fact that they may carry heavy burdens, they are consistent and dependable. They are the ones who keep the ship running smoothly. Where would you or your organization be without them? Their contributions are priceless. Ensure they know it.

4. Ask. Ask. Ask. While they would do a great job, Steady Gliders rarely seek out opportunities or additional assignments. They aren't going to scream, "Pick me. Pick me." or "Let me. Let me."

They may lack confidence, fail to see their talents or simply be unwilling to call attention to themselves. Ask them to try new things. Ask them to stretch. Ask them to take on new assignments and roles. Just don't be surprised or offended if they are resistant or say no.

5. **Encourage them.** Sometimes all a Steady Glider needs is a bit of encouragement as they take on something new and challenging. Gently remind them of the skills they possess.

My Steady Glider sister has been asked numerous times to lead new projects at work. It stresses her out immensely each time she is put in charge of a new program. She worries about doing it right and whether she is up to the task, but she always delivers.

Empower Steady Gliders when they are racked with uncertainty by telling them the qualities you see in them, that you believe in them, and that you know they will succeed. Remind them of when they successfully pushed through previous challenges they now are able to do with ease.

6. **Provide direction and keep tabs on how things are going.** While they work hard and want to please you, Steady Gliders tend to need more direction than their High Flyer cousins when acquiring new skills and taking on new projects.

Patiently provide what they need and they will be golden. Refrain from assuming they know exactly what you want and that they will hit it out of the park. Check in on their progress and provide corrections before they veer too far off course.

7. Recognize their courage and efforts when they try new things. When a Steady Glider steps up for you or for themselves, acknowledge the courage it takes to try new things. Recognize the efforts they are making as they push themselves and take risks.

Steady Gliders flourish in supportive environments. Give them the gift of respecting their values. Recognize their contributions. Offer them opportunities.

Breathe wind into their sails by encouraging and supporting them as they engage in new endeavors. They will flourish and you will enjoy their undying loyalty.

Still waters run deep!

CHAPTER 4

Run The Rapids: Lackers

Are you stuck? Do you keep running into the same obstacle? Is there an area in your life you continue to struggle with despite your best efforts? Do you surge forward only to fall back time and again? Is there something you've been trying to overcome or accomplish for years?

Or, is your boss pressuring you to come up to speed at work? Are you being forced to learn a new skill, adopt a new system, or do something differently? Although you've truly tried, do you have little to show for your efforts? Are you discouraged by your lack of progress? Are others frustrated by your inactivity and inertia?

If you keep encountering the same difficulties as you try to steer your way to success, don't despair. If you've yet to achieve what you desire and deserve, don't abandon ship. What you're lacking is either a critical skill set or an equally critical mind set.

Skill sets center around knowledge and taking appropriate action. They include things like math, science, accounting, finance, foreign languages,

> Internal barriers that keep you from learning or achieving success are mind set problems.

technology, interpersonal and social skills, oral and written communication skills, time management skills and being able to fix or build things.

Positive mind sets that propel you forward include things like believing you can accomplish what you're trying to do, being open to new experiences and getting excited about learning.

Negative mind sets that hold you back include things like doubt, fear, depression, anxiety, getting overwhelmed, feeling inadequate and shutting down emotionally or intellectually. Internal barriers that keep you from learning or achieving success are mind set problems.

The pressure to overcome what holds you back may feel greatest in the workplace as you risk losing your job. However, the stakes outside the workplace can be equally high. Failure to steer past your obstacles can result in the loss of your health, your happiness, your well-being, your relationships and other things you prize and love.

As a Lacker, you face a choice. You can ignore what's tripping you up. Unfortunately, you will suffer consequences. Or, you can navigate and overcome whatever impedes your progress.

Each time you push past what holds you back, you sail to the next level. Fail to make course corrections, and you will steer toward the wasteland of dashed dreams, broken relationships and a squandered life.

I distinctly remember hitting the wall during an advanced statistics course. As I walked home from class I had an internal conversation with myself:

"I don't think I can do this. I'm going to have to quit."

"Okay, if you quit, is there anything else you want to do?"

"No, getting my doctorate and teaching is my dream."

"Well then, you better go back and see the professor."

This was a skill set problem. Left to my own devices, I would not have made it through the course. Trust me when I tell you learning statistics did not come easily. I succeeded through great effort and seeking out additional assistance. Thank you, Dr. Jim Collins, for turning the complex into something I could grasp.

There have also been times in my life when training didn't make much of a difference.

When training doesn't work, it is a mind set problem.

A bit of a mess in my first job, I was repeatedly forced to drain my energy working out of my weaker areas. The job wasn't emotionally rewarding. Even worse, I suffered from the Imposter Syndrome and constantly worried they would figure out I didn't know what I was doing. It didn't take long before I was depressed.

Knowing that I was struggling to get things done, my boss sent me to a Franklin Covey Time Management seminar. Although they provided great information and gave me expensive tools to keep me organized, it didn't change anything except to make me feel worse about myself.

When training doesn't work, it's a mind set problem.

My ability to get things done in a timely manner improved drastically once I entered counseling and overcame my depression. Finding my passion and a job that utilized my strengths also enhanced my motivation, success and happiness.

When it's a mind set problem, address the underlying reasons and you'll move forward to success. Overlook your underlying problems, and you'll be as trapped as a sailor waiting for the wind to blow.

Navigate To Success

If Lackers want to achieve lasting success, it is imperative they overcome their obstacles. We'll start by examining what Lackers can do to overcome what holds them back. Then we'll look at what others can do to enhance their relationships with Lackers and to empower them to come up to speed.

Navigation Tips for Lackers:

At risk for losing jobs, broken relationships and an unfulfilled life, it is critical you overcome what holds you back. You alone are responsible for your time, money, job, well-being, success and happiness. If you don't like where you are, use the following tips to navigate your way to a better place.

1. **Recognize no one has it totally together.** Being a Lacker is not a life sentence. Everyone is a Lacker at various times throughout their life. Being a Lacker isn't what leads to long term problems. It's staying stuck that creates calamity.

2. **Identify if it's a skill set problem.** If you're lacking a skill set, training will produce the results you desire. The good news is, you're adept at learning. You've spent your entire life doing it. You learned to walk, talk, read and write. You've also learned sports, hobbies and all kinds of things along your journey.

While it won't always be easy, as long as you're willing to work hard and you possess the necessary intellectual and physical skills, you can master anything from technology to a new language to conflict resolution skills.

> Value yourself enough to acquire
> the knowledge you need.

3. **Bring your skill sets up to speed.** One of the best parts of living in today's world is the access you have to knowledge. While some resources are expensive, others are completely free.

Steer yourself to success by continuing to read great books, attending workshops and conferences, taking classes, and watching TED Talks and "how to" YouTube videos.

What's important is that you value yourself enough to acquire the knowledge you need to be successful. If a lack of formal training is holding you back, it's time to invest in your future.

If, like me, you need a coach to learn how to be a business woman, hire one. They are worth their weight in gold. The true value of a coach lies in their ability to get you where you want to go far faster and with fewer mistakes. As with other occupations, coaches aren't created equal. Get references and hire a good one.

4. **Tell yourself the truth when an internal mind set problem holds you back.** If training hasn't worked, something else is holding you back. You may have told yourself you can't do something, lack confidence or have a mental block. Maybe you've been wounded emotionally, intellectually, physically, or spiritually.

Perhaps you're traumatized. Fear may be immobilizing you. Discouragement might be pinning you down. You may even be so used to being a Lacker you've given up on one or more areas of your life.

No amount of skill set training will overcome a mind set problem. Address what's really holding you back and you'll soar.

5. **Seek help to address underlying causes.** If you're struggling with your mental health, see a therapist. If you're struggling with your physical health, see a healthcare professional.

If you've been traumatized, work with a trauma therapist. If you're struggling to forgive yourself or others, seek a coach, pastor or spiritual advisor. If you're traveling full speed ahead except in one area

No amount of skill set training will overcome a mind set problem. Address what's really holding you back and you'll soar.

of your life such as learning technology, hire a coach to help you overcome your internal barriers.

Exercise good judgement when you hire someone and only work with highly recommended people. Otherwise, you risk taking on water or tipping your boat.

6. **Calculate the cost of staying stuck.** If you think you can't afford to work with an expert, figure out what it costs for you to stay stuck for a month, year or decade. Don't forget, the price transcends dollars. It's also measured in your health, relationships, hopes, dreams, well-being and career.

7. **Stop burning through your support system.** Most people are happy to provide short term help. If you've experienced a pattern of people disappearing, it's likely you scared them off by expecting them to take on your life tasks and to be your pack mule. On the journey of life, each person must carry their own load.

8. **Release the anchors weighing you down.** Each time you talk about what other people are or aren't doing or what isn't working, you weigh yourself down. Start moving forward by asking yourself, "What am I going to do about it?"

9. **Take action.** As the old saying goes, "If you do what you've always done, you'll get what you've always gotten." If you want to enjoy a happier life, healthier

relationships and greater success, the time for complaining has passed. It's time for action.

Regardless of what's happened to you, it is ultimately your responsibility to navigate your own life. At all costs, avoid the rocky shores of self-pity and staying stuck.

Lifelines For Lackers:

If you have a Lacker in your life, you've experienced firsthand the pain of watching someone struggle. You also know the frustration of being run ragged when Lackers attempt to ensnare you in their nets.

Here are things you can begin doing today to encourage Lackers to power past their obstacles and to keep from being sucked in by their undertow.

1. **Stay on the platform.** Rollercoaster rides end up exactly where they start. The same holds true for Lackers taking the same ride over and over again.

   The brilliant E.B. Rawls taught me her strategy of staying on the platform. Rather than wearing herself out jumping onto someone else's ride, she calmly waits for the roller coaster and rider to return.

   Staying off a Lacker's emotional ride empowers you to focus on steering your life rather than repeatedly being drawn off course. It also enables you to respond with compassion when the rider returns.

2. **Ask, "What are you going to do about it?"**
   Lackers can get stuck in the vortex of chronically
   complaining about their problems. If you're going to
   successfully navigate your own life, you can't throw
   away your time and energy by repeatedly listening to
   a Lacker's never changing story.

   Rather than giving advice that won't be acted upon,
   or running away as quickly as you can, with great
   compassion ask, "What are you going to do about it?"

   My energy levels are higher and my frustration levels
   lower since I started asking Lackers, "What are you
   going to do about it?" It's an incredible strategy I
   learned from author, blogger and friend, Linda Johnson.

3. **Refuse to care more about a Lacker's life than they
   care about their own.** You are in dangerous waters
   when you find yourself investing more time, effort
   and energy into a Lacker's life, problems and dreams
   than the Lacker devotes.

   Navigate back to safe waters by reminding yourself
   that, like you, each person is responsible for their own
   happiness, life, job, time, money and well-being.

4. **Gently tell a Lacker how their behavior impacts you.**
   Lackers often leave pain and devastation in their
   wake. It's fair to say, "It frustrates me when…"
   "It concerns me that…" "It's painful to watch you
   struggle…"

> When a Lacker is dropping the ball in the workplace, there's a reason. Help them identify if it's a mind set or skill set problem.

5. Set boundaries. Boundaries protect relationships and resources. Determine what you will and will not do when a Lacker is unwilling to move forward.

6. If you are their boss. When a Lacker is dropping the ball in the workplace, there's a reason. Help them identify if it's a mind set or skill set problem.

Once the reason is known, help them create a plan to come up to speed. If it's a skill set problem, training will work. If it's a mind set problem, they might be in the wrong job or need to work with a counselor or coach to overcome what holds them back.

While it's not your job to micromanage a Lacker, it is your job to provide accountability and ensure they do what it takes to come up to speed in order to continue working for you.

When you stay off the rollercoaster ride and keep from schlepping a Lacker's life responsibilities, you free yourself to navigate your own way toward a happier life, healthier relationships and greater success.

Full speed ahead!

CHAPTER 5

Paddle Upstream: Slackers

Are you light hearted, fun loving and spontaneous? Does it take a lot to get you flustered? Do you navigate last minute changes easily? Do you respond well in a crisis?

Do you tend to put things off? Is your preference to wait until you feel inspired to dive into a project? Do you prefer to work quickly? Are you energized by deadlines?

Do you frequently underestimate how long tasks will take? Are you easily distracted? Do you double book yourself? Are you constantly running late?

Do you struggle to follow through on commitments? Do you have a pattern of missing deadlines? Have you ever been accused of not carrying your weight? Do others feel obligated to do your work?

If so, you fit the person type of a Slacker. While you can still be highly successful, and Slacker might seem like a harsh term, it is how people view you when they feel forced into picking up your slack.

It's helpful to know that Slackers come in multiple shapes and sizes which include:

Lazy - These Slackers don't want to work and don't care that others must do more in order for them to do less.

Unaware - Generally charming and likeable, these Slackers naïvely fail to see the negative impact their behaviors have on others.

Immature - These Slackers put things off and regularly misjudge how long it takes to complete jobs. As a result, they create chaos, miss deadlines or submit subpar work.

Mature - Unwilling to negatively impact others, Mature Slackers pull their weight. In addition, they honor their commitments and complete good work in a timely manner.

Rocket - Regardless of type, the overwhelming majority of Slackers are really Rockets in need of a launch date and countdown in order to fully fire their engines and achieve blast off. Moving forward, the term Rocket will replace Slacker as it is a far more accurate portrayal of this often misunderstood and mismanaged type.

While it pains me to admit, I have been an Unaware and an Immature Slacker. I wasn't an evil person. I didn't intentionally take advantage of or overburden others,

> When you paddle around your obstacles
> and harness your strengths, you
> accomplish great things.

but I did. As a result, I created chaos, damaged relationships and lost opportunities.

Doing my mental health work and opening my eyes to how my actions affected others woke me up. While I might be willing to let myself down, I am no longer willing to send others into tailspins by creating extra work, causing chaos or dropping the ball.

Despite my High Flyer mother's greatest fears, I now proudly identify myself as a high performance Rocket who shines in my chosen endeavors. If you're not excelling yet, don't despair. If I and countless others can successfully run the rapids, you can too.

The good news is you possess incredible strengths that others respect, admire and need. When you paddle around your obstacles and harness your strengths, you accomplish great things.

The bad news is unless you navigate carefully, you risk squandering your life and talents and leaving broken relationships in your wake. You are also in danger of developing a lackluster reputation and missing opportunities along your journey.

> Whether they tell you or not, the people in your personal and professional life have needs, wants, jobs and lives of their own.

Navigate To Success

If Rockets want to enjoy healthy, happy relationships, they must overcome their tendencies to put things off and overburden others. We'll look at what Rockets can do to bring out the best in themselves. Then we'll look at what others can do to enhance their relationships with and bring out the best in Rockets.

Navigation Tips for Rockets:

At risk for broken relationships and squandering your time and potential, it is imperative you navigate your way to maturity and high performance Rocket status.

The following are tips to guide you toward greater success in your life. Greater success in your relationships. Greater success in living a life that inspires, energizes and fulfills you.

1. **Recognize your behavior impacts others.** You create confusion, frustration and resentment each time you fail to follow through, do sloppy or late work, or cause more work for others.

2. **Do your job and chores.** While your tendency might be to put things off and avoid unpleasant tasks, push through and follow through. Work doesn't disappear or magically get done on its own. People are waiting for you. People are relying on you. Don't let them or yourself down.

3. **Don't be a pirate.** Whether they tell you or not, the people in your personal and professional life have needs, wants, jobs and lives of their own. They long to have fun, take breaks and pursue their own passions and interests. Quit plundering their precious resources for your temporary gain.

4. **Refuse to take advantage of goodwill and generosity.** While it is ok to allow others to help you from time to time, it's another thing to allow or expect someone to repeatedly over-function on your behalf.

   Rather than thinking, "Who am I to stop someone who truly wants to help?" ask yourself, "Who am I to take the time and energy they need for their own life, hopes and dreams?" Then, protect them from you by carrying your own load.

5. **Push past procrastination with external deadlines.** While putting things off enables you to play, relax and think, prolonged procrastination threatens to sink your ship. Procrastination is your biggest enemy and the enemy lies within.

> Rockets who create a life they love all have one thing in common. They found their sweet spot.

Procrastination has gotten in my way more times than I care to count. In great frustration, I've repeatedly asked myself how I could earn a PhD, write multiple books, achieve the rank of full professor and still struggle with getting things done?

I partially found the answer in my all-time favorite TED Talk, Tim Urban's *Inside the Mind of a Master Procrastinator.* His hilarious and thoughtful presentation highlights the importance of deadlines.

Without deadlines to propel me forward, I row my boat in circles. Like other Rockets, deadlines energize, guide and protect me from myself and the multitude of distractions life offers.

After watching Tim's video, I discovered the commonality of my achievements is they all had **external deadlines.** I, and other Rockets, cannot be trusted with internal deadlines. Why? Because we keep moving them while we wait on inspiration or a "tomorrow" that never comes.

Do you want a clean house? Throw a party. Want to move stuff off your to do list? Go on a trip. If you're a natural born Rocket you'll be up half the night getting all sorts of things done. I'm always scurrying around packing, tidying up, doing laundry and paying bills so I can relax upon my return.

Navigate your way to success by creating firm external deadlines. External deadlines will galvanize you into action. While you may be willing to let yourself down, you won't want to be publicly embarrassed or let others down.

6. **Refrain from taking others on your ride.** Deadlines get your adrenaline pumping, your inspiration flowing and you working harder and faster than at any other time. While deadlines propel you forward in a flurry of motion, they have the opposite effect on others, especially High Flyers.

When working with someone who feels safest when tasks are completed in advance, it will always be easier for you to accommodate their needs than to ask them to hang on to your ride in terror. They will spend days, months or years trying to fully recover. It's never worth the price.

7. **Search for what energizes, inspires and is emotionally rewarding to you.** Rockets who create a life they love all have one thing in common. They found their sweet spot.

> Set your course to what uniquely
> inspires and energizes you.

Unlike natural born High Flyers, you are never going to be driven to excel at everything you do. Your task is to find what you love. Seek it like buried treasure. Once you find it, watch out. You'll work harder and longer than anyone to achieve it.

8. **Power through boredom.** View life's tedious tasks and the things you must do as the price of the ride. Powering through boring things like a class that holds no interest is what enables you to get where you want to go. There will be pain in your gain.

9. **Reward yourself with play.** If you put in long hours with little reward or time for fun, you will find yourself working more slowly and starting to drag through the days. A gray cloud will hang over your head, and you'll find yourself increasingly demotivated, discouraged and resentful.

The antidote is making time to play. Do something that energizes you. You don't expect your phone to work once the battery is drained. Nor do you expect your car to run on empty. Don't expect yourself to perform at high levels if you don't feed your spirit of play. It's your primary energy source.

Just don't play at someone else's expense.

Steer clear of unnecessarily frustrating others.

You are different than, not less than, High Flyers and Steady Gliders. You bring unique and needed and gifts to the world.

Set your course to what uniquely inspires and energizes you. Steer clear of unnecessarily frustrating others. Utilize external deadlines to fire up your engine. There is little you can't accomplish.

Lifelines for Rockets:

While they can be incredibly frustrating in their weaker forms, natural born Rockets who navigate their way to maturity have a great deal to offer you.

Before you resign yourself to having to live with them "as is", write them off in disgust, or get angry and engage in Hacker behaviors, chart your course to success with the following tips.

1. **Recognize and utilize their strengths.** Before you're tempted to think Rockets bring nothing to the table and should be voted off the island, consider their strengths.

   Rockets can be highly effective and efficient. Set a firm deadline in front of them and they will blast off.

> Poking and prodding a Rocket creates resistance and resentment. Bring out the best in them by clarifying expectations and holding firm deadlines.

They are also highly adaptable and resourceful by nature. Their ability to quickly assess a situation, turn on a dime, and make lemonade out of lemons is often astonishing to watch. Sadly, their brilliance and contributions are often overlooked and quickly forgotten.

When motivated by a looming deadline, Rockets have an amazing ability to focus, single-mindedly stay the course, and produce outstanding results.

When motivated internally by something they want, they work as hard, if not harder, than any other type to achieve it.

2. **Hold Rockets accountable.** Saying or doing nothing when a Rocket drops the ball, fobs off their work, or isn't pulling their weight does nothing to create change. Silence says, "Everything is fine." Rather than helping, silence emboldens and encourages Rockets to keep doing what they are doing.

Respectfully and calmly say things like:

"I'm frustrated that you missed the deadline. I need for you to turn things in on time."

"It's your turn to…"

"My plate is already full, I'm going to need for you to follow through on…"

3. **Implement quality control.** If the work they do or submit isn't up to par, give them feedback and have them bring it up to speed.

   I'll let you in on a Rocket secret. When they think something is probably good enough, they will often submit it. If it's acceptable, they are free to move on. If it's not up to par, they get suggestions and are able to make needed adjustments.

4. **Avoid picking up their slack.** Picking up a Rocket's slack trains them to be irresponsible. While often painful, what motivates a Rocket to mature is suffering the consequences and embarrassment of their actions or lack thereof.

   I'm not advocating belittling or publicly shaming a Rocket. I am suggesting you let things run their natural course. Consider how utility companies utilize this principle. They provide warnings. If nothing changes, they shut off services. Once they receive payment, they restore services. It works.

5. **Clarify expectations.** With a Rocket, it is necessary to clarify what needs to be done, when it needs to be completed and who is doing it. The clearer the expectations on the front end, the greater the likelihood of success.

   Respectfully request what you need or would like to see happen. If they don't agree, don't expect things to get done.

6. **Set and hold deadlines.** Unless they are lazy or depressed, Rockets are activated and energized by deadlines. Don't treat them like a High Flyer by telling them, "I'd like it by Friday, but don't worry if you can't get it done." The Rocket will hear, "No biggie, relax. Go have some fun."

   If you must have something by Friday, successfully navigate a Rocket by setting a deadline that provides you with a buffer zone should they drop the ball. Firmly say, "I need that on my desk by Thursday at noon."

7. **Don't panic when a Rocket doesn't immediately start working on a task.** Rather than starting right away and working steadily, Rockets prefer to put things off in order to ponder various options and solutions. Quickly approaching deadlines are what activate, energize and propel Rockets to finalize their thoughts and work most efficiently and effectively.

Instead of taking a job back or giving it to an already overburdened High Flyer when a Rocket doesn't immediately start on it, set and hold a deadline that provides you breathing room if the ball gets dropped by their immaturity or inability to accurately estimate how long it will take.

8. Refrain from poking or prodding. Poking and prodding a Rocket creates resistance and resentment. You bring out the best in them by clarifying expectations and setting firm deadlines. Once you've done this, allow them freedom to determine how and when they approach a task.

While Rockets might scare you and you may never want to live their life, they will probably astonish you with what they can accomplish in a short amount of time.

Left unchecked, Lazy and Immature Rockets wreak havoc and leave a trail of disappointment and frustration in their wake. Mature Rockets enhance lives, relationships and workplaces.

Clarify expectations. Enforce deadlines. Allow Rockets the freedom to approach tasks in a way that utilizes their strengths. Master all three approaches, and you'll never have to exhaust yourself paddling upstream again.

The coast is clear!

CHAPTER 6

Hurricane Warning: Hackers

Do you ever lose your temper? Do you say things in frustration or anger that you later regret? Do you ever take jabs at someone or use sarcasm to make your point? Do you talk about people behind their backs?

Do you go out of your way for certain individuals so they will be indebted to you? Do you try to cause problems between people? Do you strive to create a sense of imbalance? Do you tell well-placed lies? Do you like creating "drama"? Do you strategically plant seeds of discontentment and doubt?

Is pushing people's buttons sport for you? Have you ever been accused of bullying or engaging in emotional or physical abuse?

If you answered yes to the first set of questions, don't despair. You, like the vast majority of individuals who engage in Hacker behaviors, do so when you are tired, stressed, hungry, frustrated, hurt or angry. While your Hacking behaviors are destructive, you can learn new skills and steer clear of causing damage.

If you answered yes to the second and third set of questions, the devastation you leave in your wake is staggering. Deliberately causing and delighting in chaos and destruction is a signal of poor mental health. While you definitely can change, you have your work cut out for you.

There are three types of Hackers:

Lacker Hackers – These Hackers are often stressed, tired and lack conflict resolution skills. Without the necessary mind or skill sets to address and resolve problems they alternate between silently seething, taking jabs at people and blowing up.

Hidden Hackers – While everything may look great on the surface, Hidden Hackers actively try to cause problems by dropping innuendoes, lying, and undermining people when they aren't present. Like rocks under murky water, they lie undetected. Running into one can cause significant damage.

Overt Hackers – These Hackers create chaos and fear by exploding, attacking, belittling, making snide remarks and being aggressively defensive of their behaviors and stances. Toying with people for sport, lying, stealing and sabotage are additional weapons in their arsenal.

There are individuals who, in their current state, simply don't care about people, relationships or the wreckage they leave in their wake.

> There are individuals who simply don't care about people, relationships or the wreckage they leave in their wake.

Navigate to Success

If you engage in Hacker behaviors you are in jeopardy of being viewed as a loose cannon, missing out on opportunities and potentially losing your job and important relationships.

If you have Hackers in your life, you are at high risk for elevated stress and burnout. You are also in the dangerous waters of being manipulated, harassed, bullied and abused. The toll on your emotional and physical well-being is high. You need to be equipped.

We'll start by exploring what Hackers can and need to do to disentangle themselves from their damaging behaviors. Creating healthier and happier relationships where problems are respectfully addressed and resolved will lead to greater happiness and success for all parties.

Then we'll transition into examining what you can do to bring out the best in Hackers, and ways to enhance your relationships while protecting yourself from destructive behaviors.

Navigation Tips for Lacker Hackers:

At risk for damaging yourself, others and your relationships, it is imperative you take care of yourself and that you develop the mind set and skill sets you need to address conflicts civilly and create win-win solutions.

1. **Create a buffer zone.** Taking good care of yourself enables you to navigate people and situations with greater patience. When you fail to do so, others experience your wrath and frustration while you suffer guilt and remorse.

2. **Get enough sleep.** According to a study by the Centers for Disease Control, one in three American adults regularly don't get enough sleep. Make sure you get the sleep you need to graciously respond to people and life's inconveniences.

3. **Ensure you have a reserve tank of fuel.** Being overbooked, overworked or overwhelmed leaves you with a short fuse. Not helpful for you or anyone else. Create space in your life by throwing unnecessary activities overboard, saying no, letting others take a turn and asking for help.

4. **Develop your conflict resolution skills.** Without conflict resolution skills you will continue to bounce between holding your tongue, taking jabs or blowing up in anger. None are life and relationship enhancing behaviors.

> Captain your ship by doing whatever it takes to learn how to respectfully and successfully navigate conflict.

Captain your ship by doing whatever it takes to learn how to respectfully and successfully navigate conflict. Attend workshops, take courses, watch videos, work with a counselor or coach, read books... Information abounds. Just vet it to make sure what you're digesting is good information.

My book *Pick: Choose to Create A Life You Love* has been picked up by multiple colleges as an advanced communications textbook because it provides a framework for addressing and overcoming conflict.

5. **Address problems as they arise.** Instead of letting things fester and grow, initiate a discussion when problems are small. Putting off critical conversations results in tension and frustration building. What builds up, blows up.

6. **Ask for what you need.** Expecting people to read your mind and blowing up in frustration when they don't is always counterproductive. Ask nicely, directly and firmly for what you need. You may be pleasantly surprised at how willing people are to help when asked.

7. Set appropriate boundaries. As discussed previously, boundaries protect people, relationships and resources.

For example, if you are carrying more than your share of the load in or out of the workplace ask for help. If people are unwilling or unable to give it to you, you need to determine what you are willing to do in the short and long-term.

8. Apologize quickly. When you engage in Hacker behaviors, you negatively impact others. Be quick to take responsibility, apologize and assure them you will do better in the future.

As you take care of yourself, develop strong conflict resolution skills and hold appropriate boundaries, you will successfully steer clear of the turbulence created by silence, jabs and blow ups.

Navigation Tips for Hidden and Overt Hackers:

If you find yourself engaging in Hidden and Overt Hacking behaviors, something has gone awry in your life. You've been wounded, hurt and let down by others. You weren't taught healthy relational and coping skills. You aren't living a life you love and instead of focusing on creating that, you turned your energy toward wreaking havoc with others.

Despite of what has happened to you and regardless of what you've been taught, if you are living life as a

Hidden or Overt Hacker you deserve better. So do the people around you.

If you desire lasting success and rewarding relationships, you must quit leaving a hurricane sized swath of destruction in your wake. The best thing you can do is to immediately begin working with a good counselor.

Dr. Allen Godwin, author of *How To Solve Your People Problems: Dealing With Your Difficult Relationships* identifies five reasoning skills needed for creating healthy, nonmanipulative relationships: empathy, humility, awareness, responsibility and reliability.

You will have to dig deep, be vulnerable and work hard. With courage and vulnerability, you can do it.

Develop these skills and you will transform your life. Develop these skills and you will enhance your relationships. Develop these skills and the world will be a better, safer place.

Lifelines for Lacker Hackers:

If you have a Lacker Hacker in your life, you are forced to walk on eggshells which is neither fun nor productive. Set them and yourself up for success with the following suggestions.

> If you lack the power or willingness
> to solve a problem, don't make things worse
> by continually trying to address the
> same issue.

1. **Let them know how their actions impact you and ask them to behave better when they are upset.** It's fair and necessary for you to let them know when they hurt and frustrate you.

   Say something like, "It hurts and angers me when you yell at me. I need you to tell me what you need without attacking me."

2. **Set boundaries.** If they persist in bad behaviors, say something like, "While I'm happy to work through this with you, I'm not willing to be berated. Let's talk once we're able to have a civil conversation." Then, walk to another room.

   If they follow you, ask them to stop. If they are unwilling to quit, leave for a while. At any point, if you are in physical danger, immediately call 911.

3. **Try to problem solve, but be prepared to problem manage.** If knowing how their actions impact you and setting boundaries don't bring about positive changes, assess if you are in a position to problem solve or if you need to problem manage.

Any time you can solve the problem, I encourage you to do so quickly. When a friend started swiping at me, I asked her to stop on two different occasions. "While I'm happy to work through what's bothering you, it's frustrating and hurtful when you take jabs at me." She apologized, but the behavior continued.

The third time she did it, I added, "I've talked with you about this twice. If you do it again, I'm not going to stay friends with you." I'm happy to report that over 20 years later we are still friends.

If you lack the power or willingness to solve a problem, don't make things worse by continually trying to address the same issue.

Manage the problem by doing what you need to take care of yourself and to minimize the damage of a Lacker Hacker who is unwilling to change.

While necessary, it takes a great deal of courage to confront Lacker Hackers. As Dr. Brenda Freeman says, "Bad behavior left unchecked grows." They can and need to do better. You deserve better too.

Lifelines for Hidden and Overt Hackers:

If you have Hidden or Overt Hackers in your life, you need to develop an all hands on deck approach in order to successfully navigate them. Like the Titanic, you are steering in a dangerous sea of icebergs.

> You can cut Hidden and Overt Hackers out of your life if you are willing. Sometimes the healthiest thing you can do is terminate a toxic relationship.

Hackers have wreaked havoc throughout time from agitators to despots and dictators, to family antagonizers, to power trippers, to school yard and workplace bullies. A portion of the population lacks the mind set or skill set to develop heathy relationships. Don't treat them as if they do.

1. **Ask for what you need.** While it generally doesn't work, the best place to start is by asking for what you need. The key is to refrain from running into the same wall by repeatedly trying to resolve conflicts with a Hidden or Overt Hacker unwilling to change their behaviors.

2. **Problem solve when possible.** If you are in a supervisory position, unless they have protected status, you possess the power to problem solve. Start by securing the support of your boss. Then, work with Human Resources to ensure you follow procedures.

   Call Hackers on their inappropriate behaviors, and clearly state they will not be tolerated. Hopefully they will change and become better people in the process.

Follow the lead of the courageous boss who told his employee that she needed to address her anger issues, or they would no longer require her services. Highly motivated, she entered counseling, kept her job and became a much happier person.

While it is easiest with a clear line of supervision, you also have the power to problem solve in your personal life by setting boundaries. You can cut Hidden and Overt Hackers out of your life if you are willing. Sometimes the healthiest thing you can do is terminate a toxic relationship.

3. **When you can't problem solve, problem manage.** Even when you recognize the destruction and high price a Hacker is extracting personally or professionally, you may be unwilling or unable to let them or the relationship go.

Problem management in the workplace might include giving Hackers less important responsibilities, having them work from home or not letting them interact with clients.

In personal relationships, problem management might include limiting your time with them, not inviting them into your home, steering clear of topics that start arguments or extracting yourself when they start engaging in abusive behaviors. Head things off at the pass by refusing to be drawn into unproductive arguments.

> Shut down abusive conversations in the workplace by saying, "The tone of this conversation is no longer professional in nature."

4. **Tell yourself the truth.** There are Hackers who have no inclination or desire to stop engaging in destructive behaviors. They lack the ability to create healthy, nonmanipulative relationships.

   Conflict resolution skills are never going to work with them. When you treat them as though they care about relationships and are capable of creating win-win solutions, you steer yourself straight into an ongoing state of turmoil.

5. **Understand their motives.** Whether they are doing it behind your back or out in the open, Hidden and Overt Hackers seek to control and manipulate people and situations in order to meet their wants and needs.

6. **Realize they can be intentionally ruthless.** Consider some of the things Hidden and Overt Hackers have said:

   "I get rid of anyone I'm jealous of."

   "It's fun to get people upset and frustrated."

"I go out of my way to ensure people are in my debt."

"I like pitting people against each other."

7. Recognize that people are often sport for them.
Like a cat playing with a mouse, they toy with people. They take perverse delight in upsetting individuals and making the life of their target miserable.

Steer clear of their destructive dance by refusing to take their bait. Rather than engaging in the same argument over and over, go silent. Distance yourself as much as possible physically and emotionally.

Shut down destructive conversations in your personal life by leaving the room or house. Say something like, "I'll be happy to talk about this when we can discuss it civilly."

Shut down abusive conversations in the workplace by saying, "The tone of this conversation is no longer professional in nature." If they persist, walk away.

8. Be on guard when someone instantly buddies up to higher ups. Long before you realize there's a competition, Hidden and Overt Hackers have run the table by currying favor with people more powerful than you. They do it to fast track their careers or status, and for protection.

> Refuse to allow unhealthy individuals intent on causing problems to commandeer your ship. Your dreams, relationships and life satisfaction are far too important to squander.

They ingratiate themselves by adopting their boss's hobbies and interests, becoming friends with their spouse, bringing their children presents... No method is off limits.

9. **They rewrite truth and history.** Incredibly persuasive, they are great at telling their version of events.

When I was a professor, I served on the university's grievance committee. A faculty member told us all the horrific, unfair things her department chair had done. I remember thinking, "If even 10% of this is true, it's bad."

When the chair addressed her grievances one by one, he provided a remarkably different story that he backed up with documentation. The committee ruled in his favor. Had he stayed silent, all of us would have believed her and demonized him.

Hackers exist. Problem solve whenever possible, but move quickly to problem management when you can't.

Limit their access to you. Refuse to allow unhealthy individuals intent on causing problems to commandeer your ship. Your dreams, relationships and life satisfaction are far too important to squander.

Safe passages!

Conclusion

You now hold the compass for new ways of understanding and interacting with others. You possess new strategies you can immediately implement for steering toward a happier life, healthier relationships and greater success for yourself and others.

You are not on a short, one day jaunt. You are on a long, sometimes treacherous journey. Navigate your life and relationships well and you will reap great rewards. Navigate them poorly and you will encounter costly damages and delays.

When you enter stormy seas, use the information you have learned about yourself and others to sail toward calmer waters. When you encounter icebergs, don't ignore them or hope they will magically melt. Slow down. Carefully steer your way around and through things that threaten your well-being and safety.

Honor how you are wired. Respect that while others are different than you, they are not less than you. Refrain from raining on their parade or belittling their values and journey.

Work to bring out the best in yourself and others. Do what you said you would do in the time frame you said you would do it.

Refrain from taking advantage of anyone's generosity and willingness to help you. Refuse to make someone else's life harder in order to make yours easier.

When you find yourself engaging in Hacking behaviors, tell yourself the truth. You are angry, frustrated or resentful. Rather than dropping hints and taking things out on others, work to resolve the problem. Ask for what you need and set appropriate boundaries.

You alone are responsible for your own time, money, well-being, job and happiness. Swab your deck and maintain your ship, and it will serve you well. When you passively let maintenance slide, problems can quickly grow into major troubles. A capsized ship can't sail.

It won't always be smooth sailing. As you skillfully navigate yourself and other High Flyers, Steady Gliders, Lackers, Slackers (Rockets) and Hackers, a happier life, healthier relationships and greater success await you.

Acknowledgements

Books and ideas are never created in isolation. I've been blessed to receive help from so many individuals.

To E. B. Rawls, I am profoundly grateful for our friendship and the insights I've gained through the countless hours we've spent conceptualizing relationships. Thank you for helping name the five types. Your creativity knows no bounds.

To Dr. Suzanne Dugger Hobson, I'll never forget sharing about Hackers with you in a Montreal café and you saying, "You either problem solve or you problem manage." What an insightful, life and relationship enhancing statement.

To the other individuals who have influenced my understanding and concepts of healthy relationships including Dr. Brenda Freeman, Dr. Ken Coll, Dr. Gary Chapman, Dr. John Townsend, Dr. Henry Cloud, Dr. Allen Godwin, Dr. Carol Dweck, Dr. Brenè Brown, Dr. Terry Rawls, Linda Johnson and Tim Urban.

To Marty Somberg, thank you for hanging in there with me and getting the book ready for publication on such a tight deadline. I couldn't have done it without you.

To the book party crews, I enjoyed seeing each of you reading *Navigate*. It is a much better book because of your honesty, encouragement and insights. Thank you, Dr. Crina Tarasi, Debbie Lukens, Nancy Tilmann, Sonja Wood, Lori Driessnack, Nancy Barnes, Anita Gross and Amy Jones.

Thank you, Beverly McHenry, my High Flyer mother. Your proof reading and insights were invaluable. Your and Dad's encouragement, help and support kept me moving forward.

Thanks also to Charlene King, who in addition to being the world's best parade and confetti thrower, is also a great proofreader.

Thank you, Nancy Vogl, for your insights and always making time for me. Thank you, Renee Papelian, for your encouragement, support and eagle eyes. Thank you, Dr. Jennifer Cochran, for your eagle eyes as well.

Thank you, Dr. Jill Howard, Frannie Medders, Tracy Oneale, Leatha Olson and everyone else who encouraged and supported me throughout this journey.

To each and every one of you, and the individuals who graciously let me interview them, my gratitude abounds.

About the Author

 Dr. Sherene McHenry, The People IQ Expert™, is a thought-provoking, high energy speaker and author who empowers and equips others to immediately begin to think and act differently.

Always a keen observer, Sherene began offering relationship insights and tips to adults before she learned how to drive. It's little wonder she was motivated to earn her PhD in Counseling from the University of Wyoming.

A former full professor who for almost two decades taught graduate students before leaving the academy to speak and write full-time, Sherene also holds a M.Ed. in Higher Education from the University of South Carolina and a B.S. in Business from Wingate University.

Sherene is also the author of *Pick: Choose to Create a Life You Love*, *The Busy Student's Guide To College and Career Success* and a leadership and workplace issues magazine column. She's been cited in numerous publications including the Wall Street Journal, Speaker Magazine and Counseling Today.

Authentic, quick-witted and engaging, Sherene is an international speaker for business, professional, and academic organizations. She provides fresh perspectives and doable tactics that minimize miscommunications, decrease frustrations, and reduce burnout.

Learn more about how Sherene can boost your organization's People IQ™ and increase your purpose, productivity and profitability.

Phone: 989.621.3763
Email: info@sherenemchenry.com